Bertha Benz

Written by Fiona Tomlinson

Illustrated by Martin Bustamante

Collins

Karl Benz invented the petrol-powered car in 1885.

Karl Benz

It was the same shape as a cart, but it had no reins.

Karl Benz took the car for short trips, but Mrs Bertha Benz took it away on a long trip.

Bertha Benz

Bertha and her children went to stay with Bertha's mum.

It was a long way, and it took them a day to get there.

There were no streets for the car.

Bertha had to take it along trails that made the car shake.

The car did not go up hills, so Bertha and her children had to push it. It was a strain!

Later, Bertha invented a gear to make the car go uphill better.

When the car's brakes failed, Bertha made brake pads.

These helped it stop.

Bertha needed petrol on the way.
She stopped at a little shop.

The people came out to see the car.
They were amazed.

Along the way, Bertha had to fix the car. She did not have a proper toolkit.

With her hatpin and her garter, she made the car start.

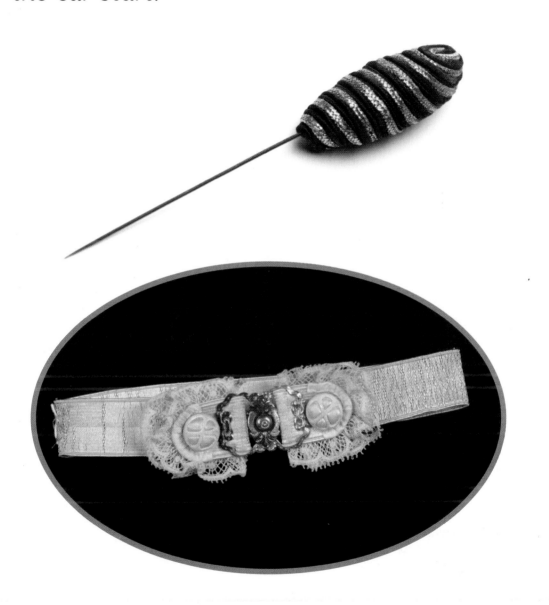

At her mum's house, Bertha sent her husband Karl a telegram to say they were safe.

He was amazed that she had taken the car so far.

When Bertha made her long trip, the car got lots of fame.

People started to take an interest in Karl Benz's cars – thanks to Bertha Benz!

The trip

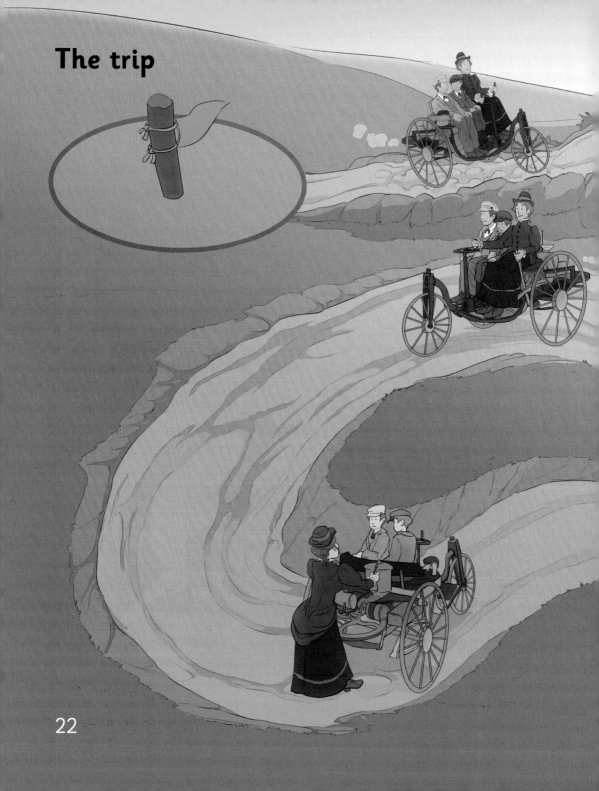

23

After reading

Letters and Sounds: Phase 5

Word count: 236

Focus phonemes: /ai/ ay, ey, ei, a-e

Common exception words: no, out, there, was, of, to, the, push, she, he, have, so, were, little, when, house, people, Mrs, these, go

Curriculum links: Design and technology; History

National Curriculum learning objectives: Reading/word reading: read accurately by blending sounds in unfamiliar words containing GPCs that have been taught; read other words of more than one syllable that contain taught GPCs; read common exception words, noting unusual correspondences between spelling and sound and where these occur in the word; Reading/comprehension: drawing on what they already know or on background information and vocabulary provided by the teacher; understand both the books they can already read accurately and fluently and those they listen to by checking that the text makes sense to them as they read, and correcting inaccurate reading

Developing fluency

- Your child may enjoy hearing you read the book.
- Read the book together, checking your child pauses for commas and adds emphasis when reading sentences with exclamation marks.

Phonic practice

- Focus on words containing the /ai/ sound. Turn to page 12 and point to **brake**. Ask your child to sound it out, then talk about the letters that make the /ai/ sound. (*a-e*)
- Ask your child to read page 9 and identify the letters used to make the /ai/ sounds in **take** (*a-e*), **trails** (*ai*), **made** (*a-e*) and **shake** (*a-e*).
- Challenge your child to read the following and look for three more /ai/ spellings. (*ey, ei, ay*)

  came   reins   made   stay   strain   they

Extending vocabulary

- Look at the car on page 2 and read pages 2 and 3. Discuss what words you could use to describe the car to someone who cannot see it. Ask:
  - What are the wheels like? (e.g. *two big; one little, lots of spokes*)
  - In what ways is it like or unlike a modern car? (e.g. *a stick instead of steering wheel; no roof; no windows; lots of spokes on the wheels*)
  - Do you think it is attractive or ugly? Why?